hair

by Sally Kindberg

WALKER BOOKS
AND SUBSIDIARIES

LONDON · BOSTON · SYDNEY · AUCKLAND

To Señor Misterioso
S.K.

First published 2003 by Walker Books Ltd

87 Vauxhall Walk, London SE11 5HJ

2 4 6 8 10 9 7 5 3 1

© 2003 Sally Kindberg

The right of Sally Kindberg to be identified as author/illustrator of this work has been asserted by her in accordance with the Copyright, Designs and Patents Act 1988

This book has been typeset in Myriad Tilt

Printed in China

British Library Cataloguing in Publication Data:

a catalogue record for this book is available from the British Library

ISBN 0-7445-9476-6

www.walkerbooks.co.uk

Why Hair?

Why hair? Because I LOVE it! When I was very little I disliked my brush and comb – I wanted wild hair like my story book hero, Struwwelpeter, who NEVER brushed his. Since then I've tried to find out why people style their hair the way they do.

Now I can tell you all about hairy show-offs, horsey headgear, a beard in a trunk, nit nastiness and much more – enough to make your hair stand on end…

go away!

Hair is Powerful

The way hair is shaped, shaved, worn wild or super-styled has always been important in some way.

Hair can scare, attract, show just how rich and important you are, that you're a rebel – or simply cool.

And hair is strong. You can dangle this book on the end of a single long strand. Weave together 1,000 strands or more and you've got a rope strong enough to lift a fairytale prince off the ground – just ask Rapunzel.

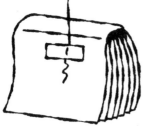

Weird Stuff

Tigers' claws, rhinos' horns, parrots' beaks, ostrich feathers and the hair on your head all have something in common – they're made from a living substance called keratin.

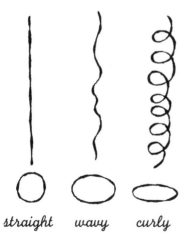

straight   wavy   curly

Humans have up to 200,000 hairs sprouting out of their heads, and it's usually on the move! Hair is pushed up through the skin out of little bags called follicles. The shape of these follicles decides what sort of hair you've got – straight, wavy or curly.

Strong Magic

Hair was thought to be SERIOUS magic in many past cultures. If hair had special powers, cutting it was a real problem in case particular gods were angered.

Badly timed combing can lead to this
(Scots, Swiss, some Native American tribes)

MENU

PRE-HAIRCUT SPECIAL

Fresh human - roasted, boiled or au naturel

(Fijians)

Save hair in roof for afterlife
(Incas, Irish, Armenians)

Stuff hair into oak tree

toothache cure
(Germans)

(British)

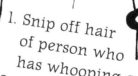

YE OLDE CURE FOR YE WHOOPING COUGH

1. Snip off hair of person who has whooping cough
2. Put hair between two slices of bread
3. Feed hair sandwich to dog
4. Person is cured, though dog may – err – bark

High Brows

stinky

tweak
tweak

ow!

ate

How to Be a Babe in Three Steps

Sometimes you have to suffer if you want to get on the beauty A-list. In the 1300s ladies plucked and shaved, poured stinky potions on their heads AND probably caught a cold at night by sitting in the moonlight trying to be a blonde babe. In Europe it was fashionable then – and for the next couple of hundred years – for women to have very high, pale foreheads like eggs, not much of an eyebrow in sight and long, golden tresses.

A bit later on, realizing moonlight wasn't doing the trick, women spread out their hair on the brims of special topless bleaching hats and sat out in as much sun as possible. Their brains might get frazzled, but if they were lucky they would get a gold highlight or two…

phew!

Oily Doily

In the mid-19th century men wore their hair short and covered it with dollops of hair oil to give it that fashionable glossy look. Their favourite type was macassar oil. The trouble was, it made nasty stains on the furniture when they leant back in their armchairs.

No problem. Those inventive Victorians thought up a good way of protecting the upholstery – they made fancy cloths, called "antimacassars", to cover the backs of their furniture.

before

after

keeps chair clean

Fancy Topknot

In Japan sumo wrestlers wear their hair in a fancy topknot which looks like a leaf from a ginkgo tree. Top-ranking wrestlers wear their hair in the *o-icho*, or big ginkgo, style. Special sumo hairdressers called *tokoyama* style the wrestlers' long hair with combs, string and strong-hold hair wax before the opponents get to grips with each other. Big ginkgo is not only a symbol of rank – it's meant to protect the wrestlers' heads if they fall over.

Toupee of Terror

Popular with punks – and even David Beckham – the mohican hairstyle was probably first worn by the Huron, a native Canadian tribe.

Scary hairstyles were always important in battle, but if a warrior had a bad hair day he could always strap on a bristly deer-tail toupee instead!

Marine Menace

Edward Teach, alias Blackbeard the Pirate, was so scary that even his own crew were terrified of him. Ruthless and cruel, he carried six pistols, was said to drink gunpowder cocktails and went into battle wearing smoking fuses in his hat. He died after a furious fight off the South Carolina coast in America in 1718.

Bigheads

In the late 1700s women started to grow taller and taller and TALLER – with the help of a lot of horsehair, some lard and a few wire cages on their heads. Massive wigs were all the rage for rich ladies.

Wigs were styled with pomade (an old-fashioned hair gel made

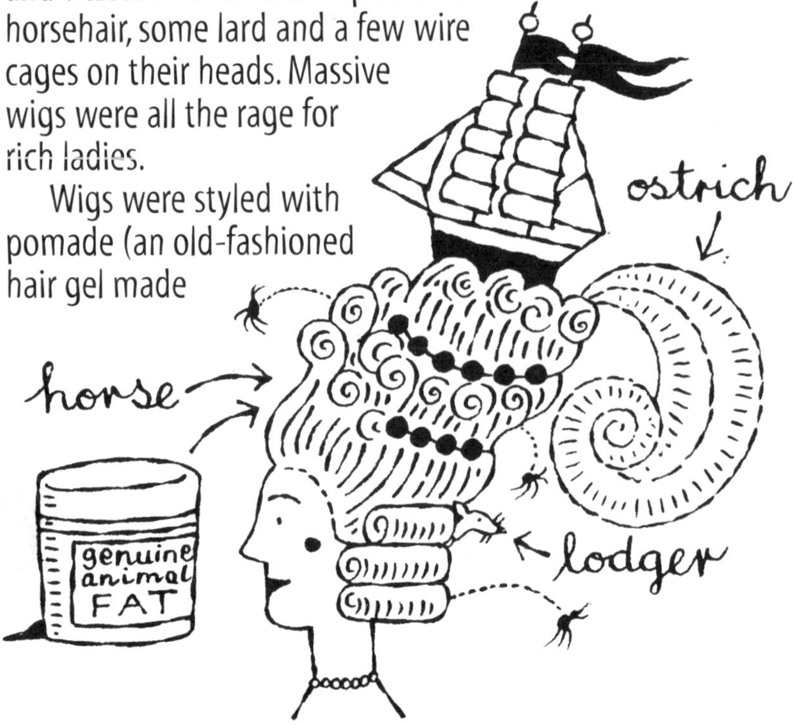

ostrich

horse

genuine animal FAT

lodger

from animal fat), then decorated with jewels, ribbons, flowers, birds — even a sailing ship or two. If you wanted to show how important you were, you had to think BIG hair.

At that time rich people travelled by coach or sedan chair, but if you had your wig on, you had to take extraordinary steps to fit inside!

Unfortunately these high-rise hairstyles often attracted cheeky lodgers such as fleas, mice and nits. Ladies used long-handled scratchers to get at awkward itchy bits, or gave their wigs a good boiling.

Macaroni Men

In Europe in the 1770s it wasn't just women who had bulging heads. A band of rich young men who'd had their holidays in Italy formed the Macaroni Club, for fashionable show-offs, in London. These dandies were so vain and silly that songs were written about them, making fun of their extravagant appearance. But did they care? Not a bit – they competed with each other to have the biggest wig.

Servant needed to powder wig with bellows

Hairspray Heights

After cans of hairspray first appeared in the shops in the 1950s, big hair was back again. Huge hairstyles could be set at the touch of a button, and bouffant hair and beehives reached for the stars. No one knew then that the gases they used were bad for the earth's atmosphere. There was frantic frizzing as girls backcombed their hair (combing it back towards its roots), smoothed it over and squirted on tons of sticky hairspray to keep it in place.

Wig Time Big Time

Wig time was big time again in the 1960s. Wigs were often cheap and cheerful and could be worn by men, women and even dogs! Anyone could change his or her image by popping on a wild wig.

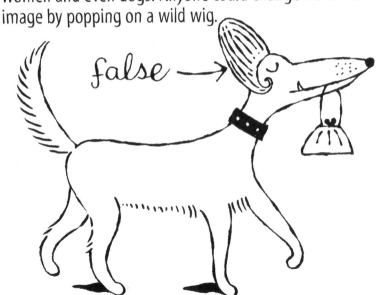

false

When UK band The Beatles had their trademark "mop-top" hairstyle (invented by a young German called Astrid Kirchherr), black nylon "Beatle" wigs sold in their thousands.

Wigs cropped up all over the place. Famous London hairdresser Mr Teasie Weasie designed a wig-covered crash helmet for cool scooter riders.

False hair was everywhere – there were not only false eyelashes, but beards, moustaches and even chest wigs for macho men.

Chinwagglers zzz

Looking after a beard can take time and trouble – in the past men have spent many hours shaping, frizzing, dyeing, scenting, and plaiting them with gold thread – even sleeping with their beards in bags at night so they wouldn't get squashed.

Nowadays a man can spend 3,000 hours of his life trying to stop his whiskers from growing.

bodkin

anchor

Amish

swallow-tail

fork

tile

hammer/T

circle

Van Dyke

Balbo

goatee

suspicious

Big Beardies

killer beard

Some beardies just don't know when to stop. In the 1500s Austrian Hans Steiniger wore his 2.75 metre beard tucked round his waist, until it got loose one day and tripped him up, killing him.

In France, Jules Dumont had a 3.35 metre chin extension. After Norwegian Hans Langseth died in 1927, his beard –

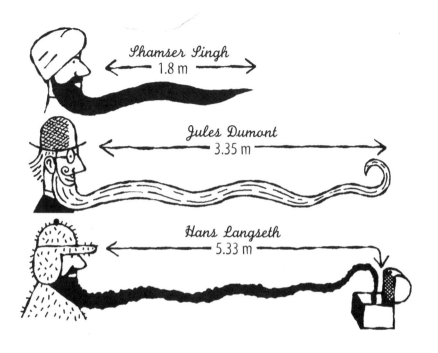

all 5.33 metres of it – was stored in a trunk and given to the Smithsonian Institute in the USA. One of today's whiskery champs is Shamser Singh from India, whose beard reached 1.8 metres by 1999. They don't grow them like they used to!

Women with Attitude

Whiskery? AND wearing a fancy frock? Bearded ladies always made the public curious, even if they were dismayed or unsettled by the ladies' appearance at the same time. Some girls, born with beards due to a medical condition, quickly realized they either had to hide away or

Clementine Delait (born 1865 in France)

Annie Jones (born 1865 in Virginia, USA)

Anna Macallame (born 1615 in the Orkneys, Scotland)

use their difference to their advantage. Sometimes their families persuaded them to join circuses, where they were paid to appear in sideshows.

Elegant Madame Clofulla, born by a Swiss lake in the 1800s, styled her beard like that of the French emperor Napoleon III. He was so flattered, he gave her diamonds – which she wore in her beard.

Top Twirlers

Fu Manchu

Dali

captain

Sherman

walrus/
soup-strainer

Zapata

toothbrush

Coleman

Menjou

boxcar

handlebar

mistletoe

major

show-off

pencil

Old Twirlers

Every month a group of men with extravagant moustaches meet in a London pub. They are members of the Handlebar Club, begun in 1947 by comedian Jimmy Edwards. There are about 100 members in the UK, European branches, and International Moustache Championships.

The club's president is Ted Sedman; his twirly moustache once measured 1.6 metres but some of it broke off during a TV demonstration – it's now 1.21 metres long.

1.21 m
when uncurled

moustache trainer

sip tea through drainage shelf

suitable for walruses

Non-Drip

Big moustaches might have been cool, but they had a way of drooping into your soup. Gadgets such as the Acme Moustache Guard solved that little problem. Serious mustachio-wearers wore moustache trainers at night to keep them looking twirly. In England in the mid-1800s, moustache cups with little drainage shelves in them were produced to prevent men from looking drippy.

Not Quite a Beard

*sideburns/
sideboards
(after U.S.
Colonel Burnside)*

*dundrearies/
Piccadilly
weepers
(after Lord
Dundreary)*

*Franz Josef
(after Austrian
emperor)*

Some people just can't make up their minds. There are styles that aren't quite a beard OR a moustache, and they're often named after the famous characters who set the trend.

*mutton/lamb
chops*

Close Shave

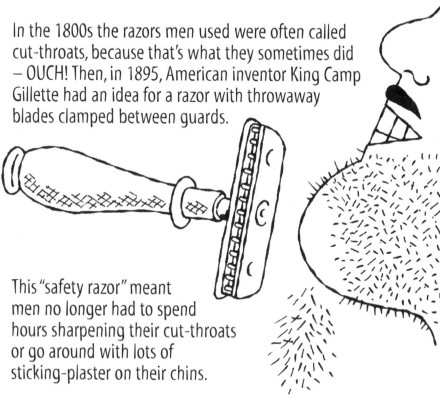

In the 1800s the razors men used were often called cut-throats, because that's what they sometimes did – OUCH! Then, in 1895, American inventor King Camp Gillette had an idea for a razor with throwaway blades clamped between guards.

This "safety razor" meant men no longer had to spend hours sharpening their cut-throats or go around with lots of sticking-plaster on their chins.

Beards Away!

Peter the Great (1672–1725) was a big lad with big ideas. The famously tall Russian emperor travelled all over Europe to find out more about the West. When he returned to Russia he was determined to modernize his country. This was bad news for beard-lovers – Peter decided that beards were so old-fashioned and uncool that he slapped a heavy tax on anyone who decided to hang on to their furry faces!

Plaits Off

In China the pigtail had been the traditional male hairstyle since 1644, so when Chinese people emigrated to America in the 1800s they wanted to hang on to their historic hairdo. However, the US thought the style was too un-American, and passed an anti-pigtail law.

The pigtail wasn't safe in China either. When the new Chinese Republic was declared in 1911, it was plaits-off time again – cutting off old-fashioned pigtails was seen as a patriotic duty, and the streets were piled high with millions of snipped-off braids.

Danger Ahead

Keeping big hair clean in the late 1800s/early 1900s was a high maintenance and risky business. The trouble was that the most popular cleansers contained petrol. This not only made your head smell like a garage forecourt, but it gave off a VERY unpredictable vapour.

After several cases of exploding ladies, it must have been a relief when short hair for women became fashionable.

honey, I'm home!

Woof! Woof!

Seen anyone lately who's hairy all over, with big teeth and anti-social habits when the moon's full?

In medieval times, spotting a werewolf wasn't such a rare event, apparently, as there were regular reports of sightings – it must have been all those long dark nights with no TV to watch. People thought these strange creatures could turn their skin inside out – one side human, the other side wolf.

Hairy Hero

Hair Star

Hairy hero Samson, of Biblical fame, was the Israelites' champion – a super-strong man who couldn't be defeated by the enemy Philistines. The key to Samson's strength was his hair. When Samson's enemies gave him a short back and sides he went weak at the knees and was taken prisoner.

But the Philistines forgot that hair has a habit of growing again. When Samson regained his hair he regained his powers. He heaved on his chains and pulled down a building, killing his enemies – and himself in the process.

Big, Bald or Twirly

(wig)

Christian nun (covered short hair)

Buddhist monk

some Muslims

some Orthodox Jews

Orthodox Greek (beards only for priests)

Orthodox Jew (side locks)

Sikh (covered uncut hair)

The way people style their hair is VERY serious business if it's an important part of their religion.

Head Power

For many years a lot of black Americans would straighten their hair to fit a white American image. But in the 1960s young black Americans grew their hair into big bushy globe shapes to show a link with their African roots and pride in being black. The Afro was a strong political statement.

dreads tucked into woolly tam

Big Dreads

Marcus Garvey was a Jamaican who started a black political movement in the early 1900s. He foretold that one day a black king would be crowned in Africa. In 1930 Ras Tafari, said to be related to King Solomon and the Queen of Sheba, was made Emperor Haile Selassie of Ethiopia. He became a symbolic leader for Garvey and his followers, who called themselves Rastafarians. Rastas don't cut their hair – they grow it into a mane of snaky hair called dreadlocks to show respect for their beliefs.

full-bottom wig

bad mood ←

Keep Your Wig On

Why do serious men and women in UK courtrooms still wear headdresses made from horses' manes? Because it was the custom to wear horsehair wigs hundreds of years ago, and things change v-e-r-y slowly in legal circles. The horsehair is skilfully looped, curled, frizzed and stitched onto a netting "scalp" stretched over a wooden block to shape it.

"baby" curl

curls and loops for wigs

barrister's wig

Judges wear two sorts of wig — not at the same time, unless they're VERY absent-minded — a full-bottom one for serious occasions and a smaller one, called a bench wig, for more casual events. The circle on top of a judge's wig represents a coif — the tight black cap worn by judges in the old days. Now it's just a tufty symbol. Before 1964, when people could still be hanged for murder, if it was REALLY bad news for the prisoner the judge would place a square black silk cloth on top of his wig.

snarl

Hair Star

Jo Jo the Dog Boy

Jo Jo was really a Russian called Fedor Jeftichew who toured Europe and America earning his living in a circus at the end of the 1800s. He had a medical condition known as hypertrichosis – his face was covered in silky golden hair. Although Fedor was a friendly young man who could speak three languages, he was encouraged to snarl and bark like a dog to please the public.

Sea Styles

In the days of sail it was important for sailors to have neat hairstyles so their hair wouldn't get caught in the rigging. Naval men scraped their hair back into a pigtail or "queue", as they called it (nothing to do with waiting at a bus stop, although both meanings come from the latin word for tail). Sometimes sailors dipped their pigtails in tar to keep them extra neat.

tar

What *do* they look like?

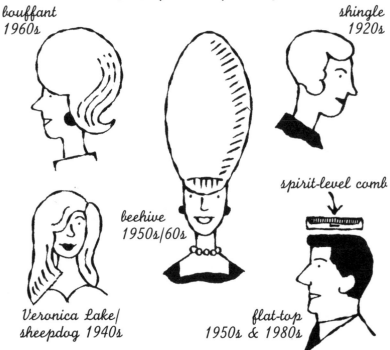

bouffant
1960s

shingle
1920s

beehive
1950s/60s

spirit-level comb

Veronica Lake/
sheepdog 1940s

flat-top
1950s & 1980s

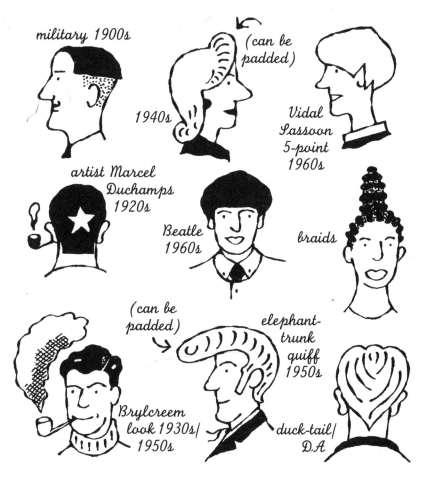

military 1900s

1940s (can be padded)

Vidal Sassoon 5-point 1960s

artist Marcel Duchamps 1920s

Beatle 1960s

braids

Brylcreem look 1930s/ 1950s

(can be padded)

elephant-trunk quiff 1950s

duck-tail/ D.A

 mod
1960s

 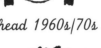 skinhead 1960s/70s

 mohican
1970s

Afro
1960s

 hippy
1960s

 Eton crop
1920s

 bob
1920s

punk
1970s

Statue of
Liberty

goth

Philly
1980s

Diana
1980s

big hair
1980

knots
2000

Caesar 1990s

razored logos/
patterns 1980s/90s

extensions
1980s

dreadlocks

ponytail
1980s

unicorn
quiff
1990s

shaved
2002/
crewcut
1950s

mullet
1980s

fin
2002

shaved/
braids/
beads 2002

kingfisher
1980

Seven Sisters

Once there were seven all-singing sisters who lived in a log cabin in America.

Sarah, Isabella, Naomi, Mary, Grace, Dora and Victoria Sutherland were also famous for their extremely long hair – its total length was said to be 10.35 metres.

×7

They made a fortune by lending their name to the Seven Sutherland Sisters' Hair Grower and Scalp Cleanser, and built a fancy mansion on the site of their old log cabin. They lived there extravagantly until the last of them died in the 1940s.

Iron On

In the mid-1960s long, straight hair was cool for girls –
so bad luck if you had curly locks! Some girls went to
extremes, and their hairdos got a bit singed – they ironed
their hair flat between brown-paper bags – STINKY! This
author admits (sheepishly) to going to bed with sticky
tape wound round her head to
stop her hair from going wavy.

pineapple   EKO, bridge   anigi (sticks)

Top Notch

For thousands of years braided hairstyles have been worn in many African countries. Hair can be sculpted into amazing shapes and patterns showing which clan the wearer belongs to, what religion he or she believes in, whether that person is married or not, and much more. Modern hairstyles are constantly changing – they can represent ANYTHING: a pineapple, a new dance, the elaborate curves of the EKO Bridge in Lagos, or simply a bundle of sticks.

Unwelcome Visitors

They cling and they swing from your hair, and they're not very nice… Yes, we're talking head lice! Head lice hatch out of little glued-on eggs called nits (each one about this size: ,) and infect around 14 million children a year in the USA.

Head lice are transparent until they've had a tasty snack of their favourite food – human blood! Then they turn a reddish-brown colour (YUK!) When they're not too busy clinging onto a single hair with tiny grippy claws, each mother louse lays about 100 nits.

But how to get rid of them? There are special shampoos which contain the same stuff that kills greenfly on roses, but some chemicals are so strong that they make the head itch more than the lice themselves. Also, some super-nits have built up a resistance to even the most powerful potions.

A less dramatic way is to use anything that makes

the hair slippery, such as hair conditioner, so that the lice literally slide off. One anti-nit website advises using mayonnaise on your head – but make sure you check your salad afterwards!

buzz
buzz

electronic nit-zapper

Old Nit

A very old nit was spotted in 1990 under an electron microscope at the University of Manchester in the UK. It was nestling up to the skull of an Egyptian mummy and was about 5000 years old.

Hair Equipment

waving
cap 1920s

Violet Ray
Generator 1925

electric
motor
hairbrush
1900s

chug
chug

hairdryer
1930s

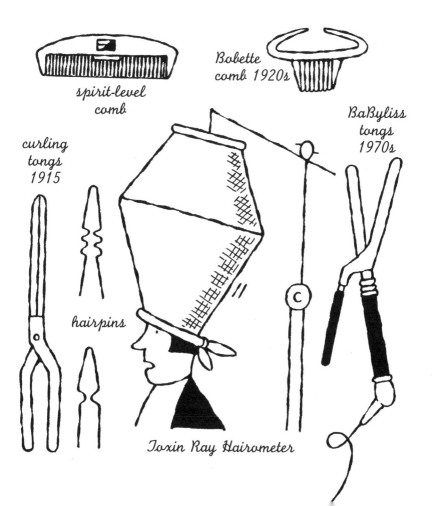

spirit-level comb

Bobette comb 1920s

BaByliss tongs 1970s

curling tongs 1915

hairpins

Toxin Ray Hairometer

self-adapting hairnet
1915

kirbigrip
1920s

hair clippers
1920s

metal roller
1960s

salon hairdryer
1930s

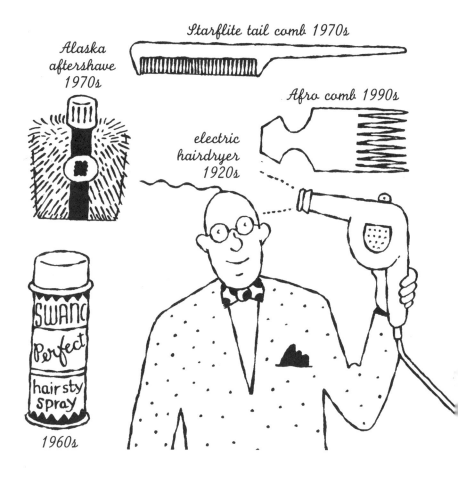

Starflite tail comb 1970s

Alaska aftershave 1970s

Afro comb 1990s

electric hairdryer 1920s

SWANO Perfect hairsty spray

1960s

Meltdown

Sitting still for ten hours wired up to a dodgy electricity supply doesn't sound like fun, but ladies in the early 1900s were willing to go through torture (and spend a lot of money) to get the new "permanent wave".

Charles Nestle (born Karl Nessler in Germany in 1872) invented the first "perm", and women queued up for the Nestle treatment. Their hair was soaked in a special chemical, wound round big metal curlers and electrically frizzed. If clients were lucky, it was only their hair that got zapped – but there were some RATHER nasty accidents.

Baldy Bits

Throughout history, men — and it's usually men — have suffered from baldy bits.

There have been many theories about what causes baldness…

Tight hat alert!

LADIES BEWARE!

no!

Too much reading can lead to THIS!

Tight hats were bad news for hair growth, according to a popular theory in the 1900s.

Some people believed a baldness bug lurked in dodgy brushes and combs.

the baldness bug

Shiny-headed men have been desperate to find a cure for their lack of thatch. These so-called cures have always been, and still are, big business.

GET HAIR OH PHARAOH

Sensitive about being a slaphead? Then rub in a mixture of fingernail scrapings and hedgehog prickles.

RUB IT IN

my mummy loves it!

Ancient Egypt

FORUM FRESH! CHICKEN POO WHILE-U-WAIT!

Ancient Rome

FROG ash

SNAKE OIL

European remedies 1700s/1800s

before *during* *after*

People still believe in weird cures for baldness today. In 1980 Mr Robinson of Maine, USA, was out in his back yard looking for his pet chicken when he was struck by lightning. He claimed that all his hair grew back afterwards.

Eventually scientists discovered that baldness was down to genetics and troublesome hormones. Once the genetic code for baldness is cracked, there's going to be a sales surge for big brushes. Meanwhile, baldness treatments have got a LITTLE more technical…

Hair-o-scope

What will the hairstyles of the future look like? Will parents be able to choose the type and colour of their children's hair through scientific wizardry? Could climate change mean we'll all grow hairier, or have no hair at all?

But the immediate future can be shaped by YOU. You've got the hair, so it's up to you to do something AMAZING with it!